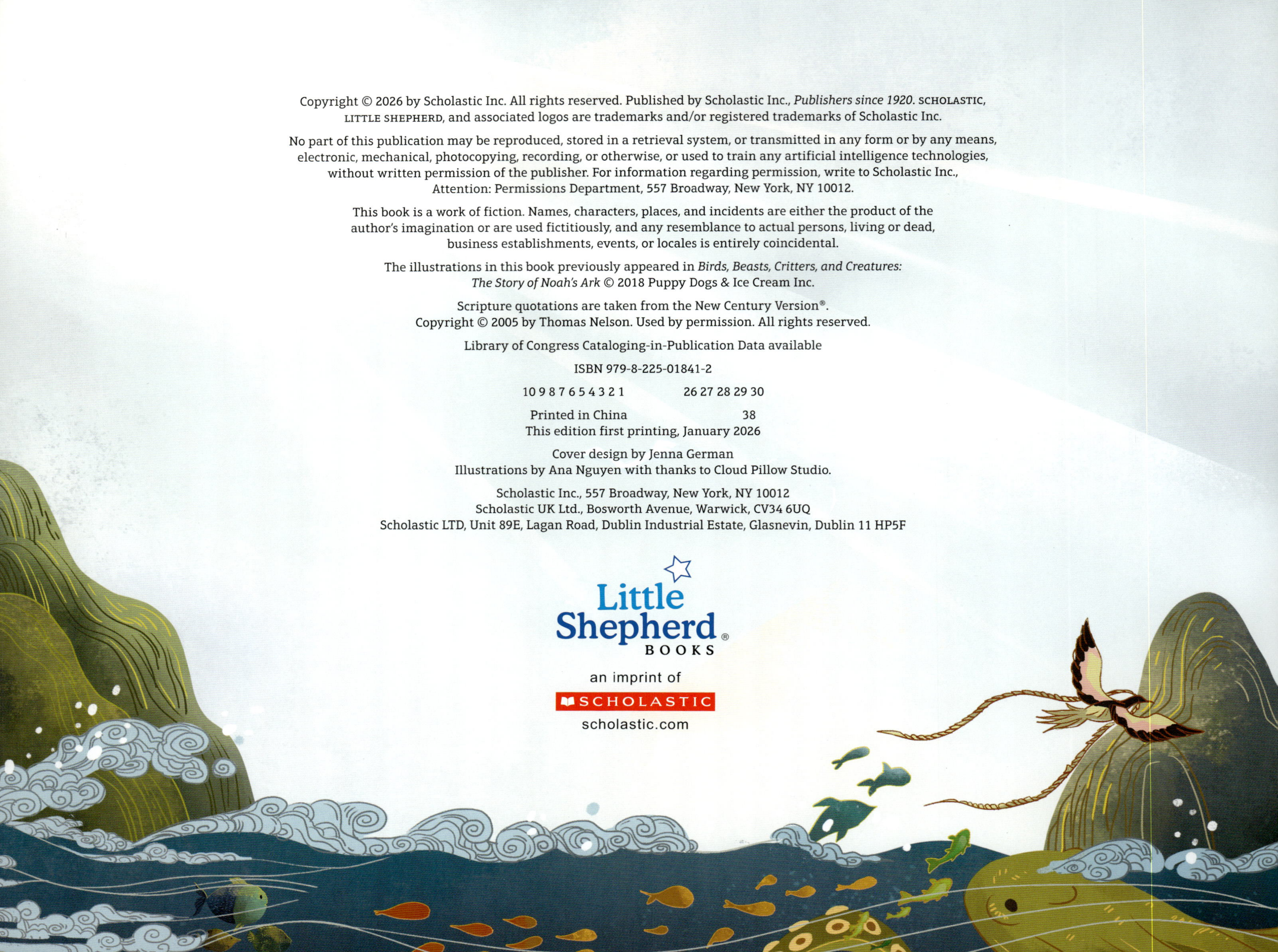

Library of Congress Cataloging-in-Publication Data available

ISBN 979-8-225-01841-2

10 9 8 7 6 5 4 3 2 1 26 27 28 29 30

Printed in China 38
This edition first printing, January 2026

Cover design by Jenna German
Illustrations by Ana Nguyen with thanks to Cloud Pillow Studio.

Scholastic Inc., 557 Broadway, New York, NY 10012
Scholastic UK Ltd., Bosworth Avenue, Warwick, CV34 6UQ
Scholastic LTD, Unit 89E, Lagan Road, Dublin Industrial Estate, Glasnevin, Dublin 11 HP5F

Little Shepherd® BOOKS
an imprint of
SCHOLASTIC
scholastic.com

All Afloat on Noah's Boat

HOW NOAH SAVED GOD'S CREATURES

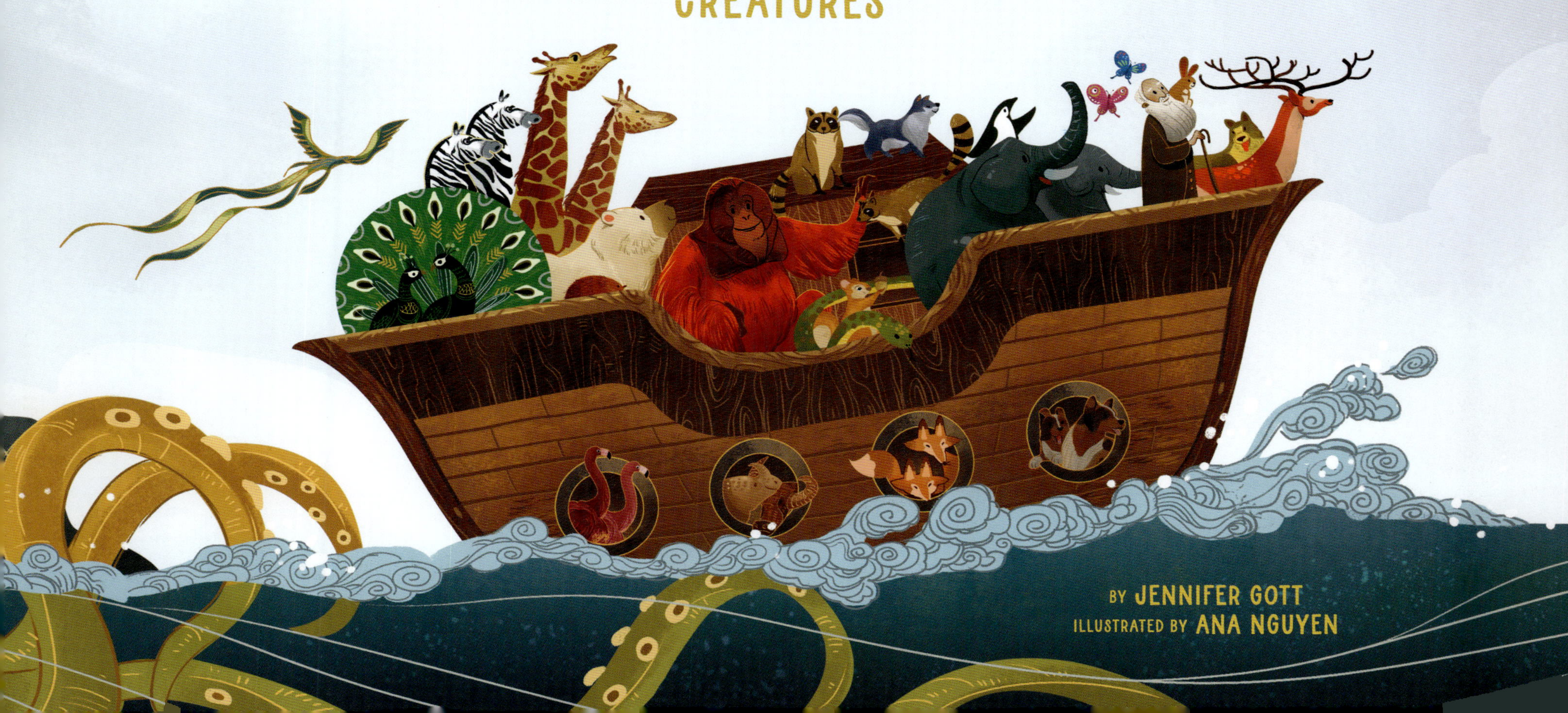

BY JENNIFER GOTT
ILLUSTRATED BY ANA NGUYEN

A man named Noah did what was good.
God said to him, “Build a boat made of wood.”

“A giant flood will destroy the evil on earth.
But your family will be safe. I see your worth.”

Noah completed the ark just in time.

He brought two of each animal—
not one left behind!

For forty
days and nights,
rain fell from the sky.
The earth began to flood,
but the ark stayed safe and dry.

Some of the creatures came out after dark.

Winged, feathered, and furry—
at home on the ark.

Tiny tabbies pounced and lions cuddled up tight.

Cats pawed and they purred under rainy starlight.

Dogs barked and played and howled at the moon.

Noah petted each dog.
"The storm will end soon."

The ark bobbed and sailed
across waves so steep,

and creatures below peeked up
from the deep.

Inside the ark, wild animals gathered 'round.
"Don't worry," said Noah. "Dry land will be found."

Through long rainy days,
birds remembered their song.
Squawk! Bok! Cheep!
the whole chorus sang along.

All the slithering snakes would slink and slide,
reptiles that coil, crawl, creep, and glide.

From forest, desert, and plains,
they all gathered near.

“God is with us,” said Noah.
“There’s no need to fear.”

The cold-weathered creatures
made their home on the ice.
Although Noah shivered,
being together was nice.

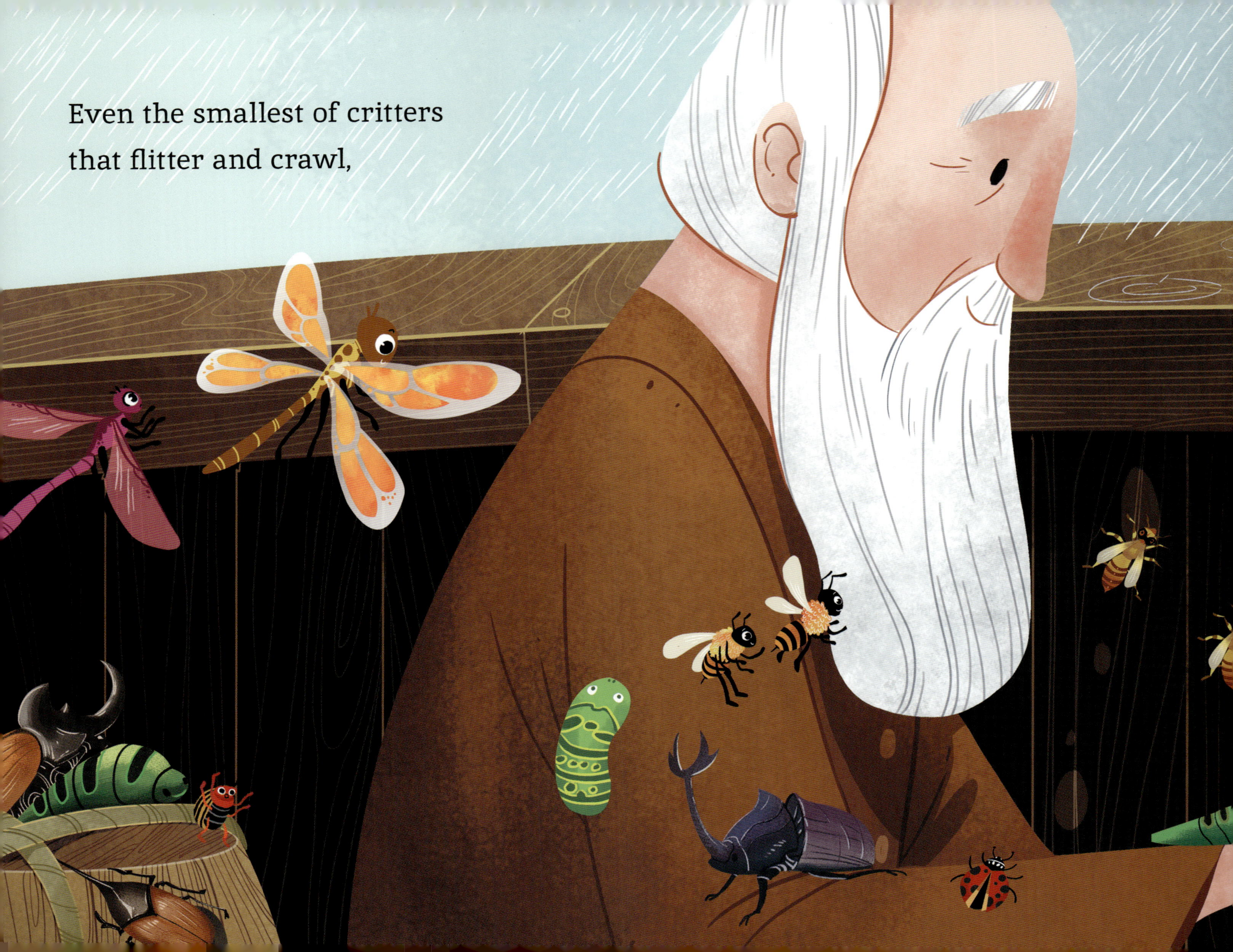

Even the smallest of critters
that flitter and crawl,

they squirmed and they skittered.
Noah loved them all.

Monkeys, baboons, and apes
climbed and played.

They swung from the rafters as the boat swished and swayed.

After 150 days, the waters rose no higher.

It was time—the earth was about to get drier.

Dry land appeared! Their journey was done.
God spoke to Noah, “New life has begun!”
“Here is a rainbow, made just for you.
I will not flood the earth again—
this promise is true.”

"I am putting my rainbow in the clouds as the sign of the agreement between me and the earth."

— Genesis 9: 13 (NCV)